I0473531

Published by:

Smart Connect

No 2 Lucas Road, Abraka

Delta State

Nigeria

DEDICATION

To Julius Ijeh, former Retail Sales Manager of FBN Insurance and current Area Sales Manager in ARMSLIFE Insurance Company.

ACKNOWLEDGEMENTS

To Julius Ijeh

I decided to acknowledge you first because you are a good and great salesperson in the field of insurance. Not that you are just a sales person but have graduated to the area of managing and guiding group of salespersons in a unit. I admire your commitment, effort, hard work that took you to the current level of managing group of unit managers in Abuja region of the Federal Republic of Nigeria. I am grateful to you because I would not have chosen insurance as a profession without knowing you. Thanks so much for your motivation in making me a good salesperson in the insurance company.

To Ekhator Godwin

I want to use this opportunity to appreciate my own unit manager Ekhator Godwin for pushing me to the level I am today as a financial advisor in FBN Insurance. You made sales so easy and something to love for all the financial advisors under you. A man that always makes his people understands that where they are today is better than where they were yesterday.

To FBN Insurance Abraka Unit

You are a formidable team of financial advisors. Sometimes we gist, we smile and we make one another angry in the office. But that is what makes us people with different characters. Thank you all for your tips and ideas. More importantly, I want to appreciate my own personal persons Nwaeke Gideon, Eiythan Stanley, and Okere Ese.

TABLE OF CONTENTS

Chapter 1

Introduction to Insurance and Insurance Salespersons

It can be so interesting to work as an agent in any insurance company of your choice. At the same time, the bitter truth is that the job can be frustrating if you are not strong enough to stand the test of time. Choosing insurance job involves a lot of maturity and understanding of the way to sustain yourself all through your stay in the job.

Students in school are thought lots of theories concerning the course insurance. They memorize many terms to make good grades in their exams and feel happy when the results are out. But little do some of them know about the real business which is getting jobs in insurance companies to work as agents after their graduation from institutions of higher learning.

Choosing and Working as an Insurance Agent

There are things which you need to know about the job before choosing it as a profession. This will prepare your mind ahead of what you will experience when you pick the offer of working in an insurance firm. The work is explained in such a way that you will understand everything in detail. It is an eye opener to guide you in your choice.

The job is a commission based job. What this mean is that you are not fixed on a basic salary like other jobs that you are paid a particular amount of money once your salary is due. This is a different ballgame. You pay yourself. You are given a blank cheque and expected to redeem yourself.

Also, there are things you have to do to get the results expected for you to climb up. One is for you to understand that insurance is not for everyone. You do not sell to the hungry. It will be abnormal for you to sell an insurance product to someone who hardly feeds three square meals in a day. If you want to increase the figure of what you earn as commission, you should be more interested in quality businesses backed up with quantity. But quality should be the first.

Your customers are the kings in your business. You have to give your customers the attention they need from you. Do not be far from them. Even if they call you in the night when you have gone to bed, answer their calls because they may have pressing needs or enquiry at that point in time. Respect them because your money is indirectly paid by them. You earn from them.

There are many tips every insurance agent needs to know before he or she can succeed in the insurance business. This is an introduction and we cannot explain everything in this introductory section. Take your time to read and understand what is written here. It will surely give you upper hand for excellence.

Before ending this subheading of this introduction, there is something basic to know. The basic thing is "sell rightly". Do not lie to any customer because you want to make sales. A customer you lie to today because you want to have productions can end up spoiling other peoples mind from buying your company's insurance policies.

So, do not lie to them because it pains when the policyholder finds out. Lie can take you to cell if the policyholder you sold to through insincerity finds out. It is important to make sales but salespersons should sell with truth.

1.1 The History of Insurance

The history of insurance traces the development of the modern business of insurance against risks, especially regarding cargo, property, death, automobile accidents, and medical treatment.

Choosing and Working as an Insurance Agent

It is important to know that insurance companies work to eliminate risks (as when fire-insurance providers demand the implementation of safe practices and the installation of hydrants), spreads risks from individuals to the larger community, and provides an important source of long-term finance for both the public and private sectors. Insurance companies generate profits and make use of such profits to develop the country where they are situated. Insurance companies have really helped in creation of jobs for people in the society.

Origin of Insurance as dated back to the Ancient Days

In the ancient days, people do their businesses within themselves. The buying and selling was just between the communities and neighbours. But this kind of business did not continue like that. There were better developments in entrepreneurship over time.

With the invention of vehicles and ships that move goods internationally, businesses began to take another dimension. Because of the international businesses, some goods get lost as a result of accident, sea storm, pirate attack, goods damage due to poor handling while loading and unloading, and other challenges. So many businesses folded because of the risk involved in transportation of these goods from one country to another.

In the course of making efforts and thinking of how to manage the risk involved, insurance was given birth to. That was how the definition of insurance was given as the oldest method of transferring risk. The risk involved in conveying goods from one point to another is transferred to insurance companies to manage.

Choosing and Working as an Insurance Agent

Marine insurance is very important for international trade and makes large commercial trade possible. The risk hedging instruments our ancestors used to mitigate risk in medieval times were sea/marine (Mutuum) loans, commenda contract, and bill of exchanges (Nelli 1972) highlighted that commenda contract and sea loans were almost the closest substitute of marine insurance. Furthermore, he pointed out that for a half century, it was considered that the first marine insurance contract was floated in Italy on October 23, 1347; however, professor Federigo found that the first written insurance contracts date back to February 13, 1343, in Pisa.

Also, Italian traders spread the knowledge and use of insurance into Europe and The Mediterranean. In the fifteenth century, word policy for insurance contract became standardized. By the sixteenth century, insurance was common among Britain, France, and the Netherlands. The concept of insuring outside native countries emerged in the seventeenth century due to reduced trade or higher cost of local insurance.

History of Life Insurance

Any event that has been happening in our society today has its origin. Also, every company that exist in the world today have their individual history. In this same regard, life insurance has its own origin. Life insurance in this history context is a contract between an insurance policyholder and an insurer or assurer, where the insurer promises to pay a designated beneficiary a sum of money (the benefit) in exchange for a premium, upon the death of an insured person (often the policyholder).

Choosing and Working as an Insurance Agent

According to College of Insurance and Financial Management of Nigeria, the first evidence of life insurance dated back in 1583 when a policy was issued on life of William Gibbons on 18th June for a 20 sum of £382 6s 8d (College of Insurance and Financial Management 2017). The insurance contract was a 12 months life insurance plan. What it implies is that if Gibbons was to die within one year of coverage, the insurer will pay the agreed sum assured at the initiation of the contract. William Gibbons died on 8th May, 1584.

After the death of the life assured, there was a slight dispute on whether the claim was to be paid or not. The argument was on whether the calculation on one year was to be based on twelve calendar months or twelve times twenty-eight days (lunar month). But after much deliberation, the claim on the life assured was paid.

Short term policy like that of Gibbons was the one in existence in those days. Today, there are long term life insurance policies. Though there are still one year insurance plans that cover the life of policy holders, insurance companies encourage their agents to sale more of long terms. Also, there is a maximum age that companies allow for prospect to enter into life insurance. As of the time of publication of this book, the maximum entry age an intending customer can enter into any life insurance policy is 64 years in respect to the life cover plan of FBN Insurance. The maximum maturity age is 65 years for the same company standard.

1.2 Definitions and classification of Insurance

So many scholars have their views on insurance. Their definitions are unique but all still centre on risk management and transfer. Also, there are classifications of insurance depending on one or two factors or points of references.

Definitions of insurance

(1) Insurance is an arrangement by which a company or the state undertakes to provide a guarantee of compensation for specified loss, damage, illness, or death in return for payment of a specified premium.

(2) Insurance is a means of protection from financial loss. It is a form of risk management, primarily used to hedge against the risk of a contingent or uncertain loss (Wikipedia 2019).

(3) Insurance is an arrangement with an insurance firm under which you pay them regular amounts of money and they agree to cover your costs if a certain unfortunate event occurs, for example a traffic accident, damage to property or illness (Národná banka Slovenska 2017).

(4) Insurance is a risk transfer mechanism whereby pure risk is transferred from the insured to the insurer, who typically is in a strong financial position to pay the loss than the insured. This definition is in view of insurance as a risk transfer mechanism.

(5) Insurance is defined as a pooling mechanism which involves the spreading of losses incurred by few over the entire group, so that in the process, average loss is substituted for actual loss (College of Insurance and Financial Management). This definition views insurance as a pooling mechanism. The principle implies that a group of people exposed to similar risks come together and make contributions towards a pool of funds. This contribution is collected by insurance company which acts as trustee to the pool, in the form of premium. The good thing about this mechanism is that risk of few people is spread over a larger group of people, all of whom are exposed to risk of similar nature.

Classification of insurance

Insurance is of many classes. The classifications vary depending on any view point applied. The three major views looked at are classification by functions, classification by main class and classification by statute. In this book, we will cover insurance classification by statute.

Classification of insurance by statute

The classification of insurance by statute is broadly divided into two. They are:

(1) Life insurance business; and

(2) General business

Choosing and Working as an Insurance Agent

Life Insurance Businesses

Life insurance business is divided into two major groups. They are investment and term insurance (also known as risk). Investment involves saving money for a particular project through insurance companies which also covers the life of the policyholder. Investment insurance policies are also known as endowment policies. There are many investment plans designed by different insurance companies. Some of these plans mature in different number of year (s). There is one, five, and six years investment plans designed by FBN Insurance but other companies also have the maturity durations for their own investment products.

Risk or term products as part of Life insurance businesses are products that insure the life of the policyholder. Risk products cover the life of the policyholder against death, permanent disability and also critical illness. Sometimes the premiums paid in risk businesses are not refundable.

If it is a one year life cover policy (risk business) that covers only death, the premium is not refundable if the insured does not die at the end of the one year. For five years risk policy, one year premiums payment can be refunded to the life insured at the end of five years if the policyholder does not die.

According to College of Insurance and Financial management, in the case of life insurance, there shall be 3 categories:

(a) Individual life insurance business;

(b) Group life insurance and pension; and

(c) Health insurance business

Choosing and Working as an Insurance Agent

General Insurance Businesses

General insurance is insurance coverage for property and liability risks. With general insurance, payments made by insurance companies are based on the loss incurred, rather than being a fixed sum as in life insurance.

Eight categories of general insurance are:

(a) Fire insurance business;

(b) General accident insurance business;

(c) Motor vehicle insurance business;

(d) Marine and aviation insurance business;

(e) Oil and gas insurance business;

(f) Engineering insurance business;

(g) Bonds credit guarantee and suretyship insurance business; and

(h) Miscellaneous insurance business.

In general insurance, the premium to be paid to cover a particular property is dependent on the value of the property. Let's take for example that a car costs $7,551 and the owner wants to insure it. The amount to be paid for the insurance is some percentage of the cost of the car. It can be 3% of the car value or cost depending on the option the car owner is opting in for. If the owner of the car later has accident with the car when the insurance on the car is still in force, he is given the cost of repair by the insurance company.

References

- College of Insurance and Financial Management (2017), Insurance Agency Proficiency, published by Chartered Insurance Institute of Nigeria, Ogun state, Nigeria
- Collins Dictionary (2016), Definition of 'general insurance', published by Collins Dictionary, New York, United States
- Dan, C (2014), Why Do Some Life Insurance Policies Have a Waiting Period?, published by Pivot Insurance, San Diego, California, United States
- Národná banka Slovenska (2017), What is insurance?, published by Národná Banka Slovenska, Bratislava, Slovakia
- Wikipedia (2019), History of Life Insurance, published by Wikipedia, San Francisco, United States, retrieved March 2, 2019

Chapter 2

Terms in Insurance

Here, we will be looking at the terms used in insurance all over the world. These are terms used in everyday businesses in the world of risk management. Every insurance agent or prospective insurance agent has to be conversant with these terms for easy communication.

Marketing

Marketing is the process of determining consumer demand for a product or service, motivating its sales, and distributing it into ultimate consumption at a profit. According to Nwaiwu, marketing is a set of activities that facilitate exchange transactions involving economic goods and services for the ultimate purpose of satisfying human need. In marketing, insurance agents talk to prospects, persuading them to pick one or two products to satisfy the needs of the prospect. The positive end product of marketing is closing of the business or simply put as production. Production is the positive fruit of marketing.

Choosing and Working as an Insurance Agent

Premium

Premium is the money paid by a policy holder to keep the insurance contract he or she entered always active. According to Julia Kagan, an insurance premium is the amount of money that an individual or business must pay for an insurance policy (Julia 2019).When there is no payment of premium as of when due, the insured will lose his or her cover. Premium can be paid monthly, quarterly, half yearly, annually or as lump sum (also called single premium).

Sum assured

Sum assured is the total amount of money a policyholder will claim at the maturity of the policy so far the initial agreed premiums are paid as suppose. The sum assured is the amount of money an insurance policy guarantees to pay up before any bonuses are added. In other words, sum assured is the guaranteed amount the policyholder will receive. Sum assured is calculated at the initial signing in to any insurance policy. If there is increase in premium as contrary to the agreed sum at the commencement of the policy, the sum assured can be recalculated. Also, if the customer defaults in paying of premiums as of when due, the sum assured can be reduced at the maturity of the policy.

Suspect

A suspect in insurance is a potential prospect. When an insurance agent sees an individual first and thinks that the person can register into any insurance product, the person becomes a suspect. This is before meeting the person. The agent suspects that the individual or the organization can enter into any of the products he sells. Please know that a suspect is different from a prospect. It is suspect that transforms to prospect.

Prospect

From suspect to prospect; A prospect is a potential new customer who is approached for buying an insurance policy. When an agent approaches an individual and begins to talk to the person to buy one or two insurance policies for himself or any other person, the person being spoken to at that point becomes a prospect. The agent may choose to market all the life products they have in their company and at the end they exchanged phone numbers. The exchange of the contacts is for the final closing of the business. But not all prospects end up being policyholders. Some prospects end up not buying maybe because of financial challenges, lost of interest or any other factor.

Customer

A customer is someone who registers a policy in any insurance company. But a customer can still be an organization. Example is when Harvard University registers a policy that will cover all the staff of the school against death. A customer is a prospect who enters into contract with an insurance company by having any of the plans designed by the company.

Policyholder

A policyholder is the same as a customer. But, policyholder is mostly used in insurance generally. He is a person or organization to whom an insurance policy is issued. In other words, a policyholder is a person or organization that is insured by an insurance company to help manage any particular risk. As account holders are to bank so are policyholders to insurance. Active policyholders are the strength of insurance companies.

Insured

An insured is any individual or group whose life is covered by an insurance company. The person who obtains or is otherwise covered by insurance on his or her health, life, or property is the insured. He is the person who transfers a risk to an insurance company to stay safe in case of a contingent or uncertain loss. According to Prem Jhamnani of Insurance Institute of India, an insured is a person who is the buyer of the insurance policy (Prem Jhamnani 2018). Customer, policyholder and the insured are used interchangeably in insurance. But a policyholder is not always the insured. Example, a man can pick an investment policy in an insurance company to insure the education of the children. In this case, the insured is the education of the children.

Insurer

An entity which provides insurance is known as an insurer, insurance company, insurance carrier or underwriter. An Insurer is a company who sells insurance policies. Insurer is the one who bears the risk in return for consideration which is known as premium (Prem Jhamnani 2018). Examples of insurers are FBN Insurance, LeadWay Insurance, Sanlam group insurance company of South Africa, Securian Financial (Minnesota Life Insurance Company), John Hancock Life Insurance of United States, Haven Life of United States, and ICICI Prudential Life Insurance of India. These and many others are insurers.

Beneficiary

A beneficiary is the person that benefits from an insurance policy. There is primary and secondary beneficiary. The primary beneficiary is the person (or persons) who will receive the proceeds of the life insurance policy when the insured person dies (Trusted Choice 2013). Secondary beneficiary is an assistant who takes the claim in the absence of the primary. When entering into insurance contract, the policyholder can choose to have more than one beneficiary which is in other words beneficiaries. A beneficiary is the person a claim is paid to in the event of death of the policyholder. But in a situation where the beneficiary is a minor as appears in some educational policies, the claim is paid to the guardian of the beneficiary.

Choosing and Working as an Insurance Agent

DDM form

The acronym DDM stands for Direct Debit Mandate. DDM form in that regard stands for direct debit mandate form. It is a form that a policyholder/insured fills for the insurance company to be making debit from his/her bank account for payment of premium. It is an auto debit form. The debit from the policyholder's bank account can take place on monthly basis, quarterly, half yearly or yearly depending on the choice of the customer. Some customers fill DDM form for easy payment of their premiums and to maintain consistency in their premium payment. While policyholders fill the form, it saves them the stress of going to the insurance company or banks to make their payment in the insurance company's account (s). With DDM form, payment is programmed and done automatically at the date filled by the policyholder for the debit to be made from his or her account.

Proposal form

The term proposal form is the form filled by the insured to enter into insurance contract with the insurer. Note that insurer as used here can be an insurance company. A proposal form is the form completed by the policyholder when applying for insurance (123 Money Ltd 2014). Once someone signs a proposal form, makes his premium payment into the account of the insurance company he signed the contract with, the person becomes a policyholder. When purchasing insurance, it is necessary for the prospect to provide the insurer with information so that it can assess the risk. This is usually done by filling in a proposal form, often available from agents, brokers, or insurers (Isaac Ngaru 2014).

Termination

It is the ending of a policy before its due time. It is a general term used to refer to the end of coverage under a certain policy, usually due to the policy's term ending or due to cancellation. In life insurance, this term refers to the end of coverage of a policy due to the insured no longer paying the premiums. Some policyholders terminate their life policies when they are faced with challenges and in return needs the money they have saved with the insurance company. Know that insurance is not all about claim at death. Insurance has savings, investment, or endowment plans that people save their money with as well. Terminations are made before maturity of any policy. Depending on the way any insurance company design their policies, the policyholders are charged some percentage of their total contributed money (paid premiums) at termination. The reason is because it is a breach of contract when this happen.

Maturity

Maturity as a term used in insurance is the time a policy is due for claim. It is the time that a customer can claim his benefits. If a policyholder buy endowment/investment product with an insurance company which is expected to be due for claim in five years, that fifth year becomes the maturity time. Example, in FBN Insurance, if a policyholder buys a Flexible Education plan which the minimum maturity time is 5 years on March 4, 2019, the maturity of the policy will be March 3, 2024. This is when the policyholder wants to save for just five years for the education of the child. And that is the minimum duration as of the time of the publication of this book.

Due diligence form

In many insurance companies, no insurance proposal form is submitted without being accompanied by due diligence form. Due diligence form is a form that summarizes any insurance plan to the prospect which includes the maturity year of the contract, minimum premium to be paid, and the charges involved at termination in any particular year before maturity. Once a prospect signs the form and becomes a policyholder, everything stated on the form is binding on him.

He consents that he agrees with the terms and conditions of the policy once he appends his signature on the form. The form is also known as consent form. Primarily, the risk and insurance aspects of due diligence begin with an understanding of the structure of the proposed transaction (Much Shelist 2011).

Financial Advisor (FA)

The term financial advisor is an insurance agent who uses financial knowledge to sell insurance policies to people to meet a particular financial goals and he or she is assigned to a unit manager. Financial advisors are the powerhouse of every insurance company. They are the people that go out to get the prospects which after proper marketing of the products to them turn into policyholders. Insurance companies cannot function without the effective function of the financial advisors. Financial Advisors are like advertisers that make people know about the existing insurance services in any insurance company. They are sometimes referred to as insurance agents. A good financial advisor gets to know you as a person along with your future goals. The advisor explores your family situation by asking questions like, "Are you married?" and "Do you have children?" (Barbara Friedberg 2018).

Cooling off period

This is the grace period in which a new policyholder in an insurance company is given the opportunity to cancel the policy he entered and have his paid premiums refunded to him. You may want to cancel an insurance policy if you have just bought it and have changed your mind. By law, you have a minimum 14-day cooling-off period during which you can cancel the policy for any reason. If you've bought life insurance, the cooling-off period is 30 days. Many people cool off their policy when they start having doubts after signing in to any insurance policy and therefore decide to cancel it. This happens when the policy is not fully in force.

Waiting period

A waiting period refers to the time an insured must wait before some or all of their coverage comes into effect. Only when the waiting period has passed can the insured have a right to file a claim for the benefits of the insurance policy. Depending on any insurance company and the regulatory body of insurance in any country, some have their waiting period as three months. In this period, the company will not pay any death claim or death benefit to the beneficiary if the policyholder dies. According to Dan Cody of Pivot Insurance, United States, "A waiting period means that there is a specific period of time, such as one or two years, where the insurance company will only pay the dollar amount of premiums that have been paid into the policy to the beneficiaries. As an example let's say a person has a $100,000 term life insurance policy that has a two year waiting period. If the insured person passes away during those 2 years the beneficiary will only receive the total of the premiums that have been paid up to this point. In this scenario, the beneficiaries will not receive the full $100,000 payout (Dan Cody 2014)".

References

- 123 Money Ltd (2014), What is a proposal form?, published by 123 Money Ltd, Dundrum, Dublin, Ireland
- Baker, M (1992), Marketing Strategy and Management, Published by Palgrave, New York, United States
- Barbara, F (2018), What Do Financial Advisors Do? Everything You Need to Know, published by Smart Asset, New York City, United States
- Isaac, N (2014), The role of the proposal form in an insurance agreement, published by Daily Nation, Nairobi, Kenya
- Julia, K (2019), Insurance Premium, published by Investopedia, New York, United States
- Kingstons, C (2011), Marine Insurance in Philadelphia During the Quasi-War with France, 1795–1801, published by Cambridge University Press, United Kingdom
- MedIndia (2016), Sum Assured and Maturity Value, published by MedIndia, Anna Nagar, India
- Much Shelist (2011), Insurance and Due Diligence in the Business Transaction, published by Much Law, Chicago, United States
- Mundy C (2011), Enterprise risk: who knows my business better than me, Published by MCB UP Ltd, United Kingdom
- Prem J (2018), What is the difference between, an insurer and insured?, published by Quora, California, United States

Choosing and Working as an Insurance Agent

- Trusted Choice Life Insurance (2013), Best Way To Choose a Life Insurance Beneficiary, published by Trusted Choice Life Insurance, Cambodia

Chapter 3

Working as an Insurance Agent is Tough at the Beginning

The managers or top officials may cook sweet stories for you. They may tell you that you have already become a millionaire by choosing to work as an insurance agent. Your unit manager will motivate you by telling you that you start buying houses in different cities within six months or one year of the job. All these they tell you for you to be hopeful in the job. Few agents may have boost at the initial stage. But of the truth, the beginning of the job is not always easy for more than 90 percent of insurance salespersons. But you will earn good amount of money if you persevere. The earning is accumulative in the long run.

When you get your appointment letter to work as a financial advisor in any insurance company, be it life or general insurance company, just know that you have a lot of work to do at the initial stage. That is the time you know whether you can cope with the job or not. In the job, the agent is given a blank cheque to prove his or herself. So, insurance agents determine their fate when they start their jobs newly.

So many financial advisors leave insurance jobs 3 months of their appointment to do the job. After few months when they observed that what they earn as commission could not pay their transport for a month, they quit. Some get so angry to the extent that they lock their eyes not to listen to any advice their unit managers have for them. Many who left the job and later stated writing articles on the internet have left bad remarks about the job.

They got tired. They got frustrated and could not absorb any form of motivation on the job again. To some of them, they have no reason for being part of the company they work for. But with wisdom you will benefit from the job and leave good remark if you persevere.

3.1 Why Insurance Job is Tough at the Beginning

The Commission Aspect

Working as an insurance salesperson involves commission build up. That is to say that you are not placed on any fixed salary. You are the one that pay yourself. An insurance agent has no commission at the beginning of their job. That is to say that the agent gets paid the commission when the businesses (policies) he sold have been captured and converted by the technical administrators.

It takes more than a month before some insurance companies capture and convert the businesses submitted by financial advisors. Because of this, the agent lives on allowance for the time frame until he or she is paid the commission after the capturing and conversation. If there is issue on the proposal form submitted by the agent, the payment may take longer time than it suppose to. The form will be returned to the agent until it is documented properly and then returned back to the capturing and conversation team again. But with the increase and development in internet and technology, this issue is reducing gradually.

The annoying thing is that sometimes the allowance is not even complete. Some companies short-pay their agents if they did not meet up with the monthly target given to them. In that case, the amount of allowance paid to the agent is calculated using the appropriate parameter.

So, the agents do not get equal allowances on monthly basis. Irrespective of the fact that the allowance is made to cover the transport of the agents, some beginners in the company use some part of the money for their feeding at the beginning just for them to cope.

You have to borrow Money

If you are a young insurance agent that just finished from high school, if you have not asked for financial assistant from your family members or friends, you have not started. The reason is that it is hard for single young agent to cope with his or her own money when he had not worked in somewhere else or have money already before joining insurance company to work as agent.

Choosing and Working as an Insurance Agent

Sometimes when you call your loved ones to still make demand of money for feeding or other expenses, many thoughts may fill their minds. One of the thoughts may be, "which kind of job is this my relation doing that he does not have money to feed himself" The second question they may ask themselves is, "is this job this young man said he is doing for real?". They may not ask you these questions straight looking at your face as an insurance agent that needs financial help but many always have it in their minds.

Some of your friends may start avoiding your calls because they have noticed that you usually call for money. They will not understand the nature of your job. They do not know that you sow seeds first in your kind of job before you harvest. So many people do not really understand how insurance job is. They think it is normal salary job where you get paid a fixed amount of money every month. As an agent of an insurance company, try and explain the kind of job you do before you ask them for money. Tell them you will pay back once you start receiving your commission. That will build their confidence and believe that their money will still come back to them when everything becomes okay. The tough times will not continue for long time. So if you are considering working as an insurance salesperson, go ahead with it because the author of this book has been in it and he is doing well.

The Temptation to leave the Job

It will get to a point when you are tested to leave the job. In a society where there is scarcity of job, leaving the job may be a painful decision to take. While there is high rate of unemployment in the society, you leaving the job you were offered by an insurance company may be painful because you will feel bad later when you see the people you left some time ago doing well in that same job.

When you are tempted and you feel like not quitting, that makes you strong. It makes you have the heart of lion and know that following the tempting words to leave the job is not the best thing to do. Temptation in the tough time of that job is part of the job. That is the real thing about working as a salesperson in Risk Management Company in any part of the world.

Aditya who quitted his insurance job once stated "Insurance sale is a tiresome job because of daily travel and targets involved". From the voice of Aditya, he said so because he did not see the greater light ahead. Because of that, he left the job.

You may be tempted to leave your job in insurance company as an agent. But before you leave, know that there are people who are making strong five figures as pay from the same job. You do not need to quit at the beginning no matter what. The beginning is usually tough but better still you can break through as you progress in the sales. Sales persons should be strong and should not rush into conclusion fast by quitting fast.

3.2 Know that the Tough Times will not last

Tough times may not last but tough people do. Irrespective of how tough the beginning may seem, it can still be broken. As some metals which mere persons think cannot be broken ended up being melted down by furnace, other hard times can be cracked down.

The hardships experienced by new financial advisors in insurance companies have been experienced by the senior ones in the same companies. The testimony is that some senior colleagues made it and are living till today. Many have established businesses of their own from the money they made from the insurance job.

Some have bought cars and others are still buying. They did not steal the money; rather they made the money they use in buying those properties from their jobs as agents of insurance companies. If they can make it to buy the luxuries they make use of today, you can even do more than. Try and understand the job by having in mind that excellence is guaranteed.

Agents that are new in sales in any risk management company can go closer to those that have been in the job. They will educate them that the tough time does not last for a long time. Once you have good customer base and pick up, you forget the challenges. You live better life in the new state. It is about the time and perseverance.

Hard times are like a washing machine, they twist, turn and knock us around, but in the end we come out cleaner, brighter and better than before. So, insurance agents are strong people that can overcome hard times. Hard times do not create heroes. It is during the hard times when the 'hero' within us is revealed.

Reference

- Aditya (2017), I'm in Insurance Sales. Should I quit my Job? Published by Quora Inc., California, United States

Chapter 4

Getting Early Businesses

There are ideas that are needed for beginners in insurance companies to gain early businesses that will help them gain ground first in the companies they work. Ideas sometimes are passed to the juniors from the seniors in a particular area of business. That is because the seniors have had experience on what works and what do not work. That which works is what a good senior can pass to you to establish your stand at the beginning.

In this chapter, we will be discussing on what someone who has chosen to work in an insurance company have to do at the start of his job. Also, the ideas are valuable and important to people who are prospecting to work in insurance companies one day. When new financial advisors get these key ideas and practice them, it goes a long way to help them. It will ease them from the pressure of getting frustrated in the job at the start up. Agents of insurance companies will surely stand the test of time on adherence to the message passed in this section.

Most times, it is usually difficult for those that enter insurance sales as fresh graduates to get businesses on time. These are fresh persons in the labour market. They most times toil for weeks before they submit a complete and paid proposal form to the technical administrators. It is usually not easy for fresh graduates that choose to work as salespersons in insurance companies.

But the fact remains that those who have ideas on how to get early businesses stay and enjoy the job in the long run. But for those who have worked in some places especially banking and some firms related to finance, they easily fit into the job. The reason is because they have met many people in their places of work and those people can easily buy into their products. But in the other way round, the fresher can still pick up anytime.

4.1 Start from the known to the unknown

In Mathematics, problems are solved from known factors to the unknown. Little did we know that those calculations have real life applications until we grew up and made contacts in life. We see this Mathematical approach of solving Mathematics problems also apply in insurance as well. Beginners in insurance companies that want to gain ground and start doing well start from the known to the unknown persons or prospects.

In a Mathematical equation where we are given some numbers with alphabet or alphabets, in such equations, we may be expected to find the unknown which is alphabet (s), usually x or y. There are always known numbers attached to the alphabet (s).

Choosing and Working as an Insurance Agent

At the end, the x and y are found after resolving of the equations through the known numbers. The values of the alphabet(s) are discovered at the end and the student is rewarded with the deserved mark. Those that get the values of the unknown most times are tag as intelligent persons. They are problem solvers in their classrooms.

New salespersons that do not want to get frustrated in their sales of insurance products have to start from the known to the unknown. The sales of new salespersons should start from the people they know to the people they do not know. Do not say that there is nothing you can sell to them. If a beginner works with an insurance company that sells both life and non-life businesses, there must be something to sell to the people you know.

Investment products which are part of life insurance policies can help an insurance agent in a big way. As an agent, you can sell any investment savings plans to your family members. They can save for themselves, their children's future education for those that have given birth, or even short term for the house rent they are likely to pay in the next one year. There must be something to sell to them irrespective of anything. Insurance companies have numerous businesses that any member of your family; be it immediate or extended family members can buy.

For those agents that have relations that are into businesses, they can insure their business places and goods. That is their shops where the goods they sell are stocked and the goods as well. Even if they do not want to insure their shops and goods, they can insure their vehicles.

Insurance of their cars can give the insurance agent commissions that can keep him going for a long time. You have to convince those that you know to sign into a suitable contract with the insurance company you work with. That is what you gain from being related to them. They may not ordinarily like to do it but because you are close to them, they have to do it. They will have confidence that you are their financial advisor. Many policyholders enter into insurance contract with people they have known over the years.

One of the reasons behind that is because they can always access their advisors at any time. So, insurance agents that do not want to get tired in the job easily have to sell to the people they know first in a genuine way. This will make them as they receive their commissions every month which keep them going as they begin to meet the unknown through the known.

Who is that your mom's old friend that will be retiring from her service years soon? Does she work with government establishment or firm that pays pension to her workers after retirement? If they are paid pension after retirement, that is still a cool way for you to make cool cash from your job.

Because your mom you know, she becomes the known in this context. You may not know the soon to become retiree but you know your mother. Your mother which is the known can talk to the unknown whom is your mother's friend to choose annuity with the insurance company you work with.

In annuity, the balance money in Retirement Savings Account (RSA) of the retiree is transferred to the account of the insurance company. This balance can be millions of dollars. The insurance company now pays the retiree every month from the money.

Annuity is a product of insurance company. Annuity is a regular income received from an insurance company in consideration for payment of premium. Money leaves RSA to insurance company to pay premium after lump sum payment. The insurance company then commence payment of monthly annuity/pension to retiree. Annuity payment is guaranteed for 10 years in case of death (Rosemary Onuoha 2018)

Annuity business can change the life of an agent for years. So, as a new agent, you can have an early boost that will change your entire life in an insurance job. When you sell to the people you know, they can refer you to the people you do not know. Such can change your fortune. So start from the known first. They can lift you as an insurance agent.

4.2 Who are your customers?

Choosing your customers is also important in having early businesses. It is not all about selling to every living soul you see on the street. A basic thing you have to consider is who your customers are. Knowing this will direct your steps on the customers to take your products to for their consumption.

Choosing and Working as an Insurance Agent

Are you selling to students; poor women that you know can hardly eat; top officers in various offices; or civil servants? These questions you have to answer to yourself. The choice of your customers at the beginning of your career determines how much you take home as commission every month.

How much independent insurance agents make varies by how many clients they have; what type of clients (Ashley Donohoe 2018). If the large portion of your customers as an agent are mainly students, do not be surprised when you are paid small amount of money as commission. The agent does not need to be angry because he or she is the person that decided to be selling investment plans to students.

It is true that some students like to save maybe by choosing any insurance investment plan until they graduate from high schools. But the fact is that most of these students do not have basic salaries. They sometimes save from the allowance given to them by their parents. And in some months, they have many academic financial expenses to make.

In a situation like this, they will not have any money to save as premiums. If 80 percent of the students that the agent sold to have this kind of expenses to make in that month, that means that the agent is in trouble that month. He is in trouble because he will get paid peanut at the end of the month as commission. Insurance agents should avoid having many students as their customers because some of those students have not eaten. Many of them are hungry.

Choosing and Working as an Insurance Agent

The choice of customers for a good insurance salesperson should be people that have steady income. Agents should target civil servants, corporate workers and lastly businessmen and women. These are people that will always have money to pay their premiums as they specified at the commencement of their insurance policy.

A businessman may not ordinarily like to be saving money in a place whereby he will not have access to it for 5 to 6 years for example in long term endowment plans. But he can invest for his children's future education and give them educational insurance cover. He may see saving for himself as tying his business money down. But he can save for the children's future university education and insure their education as well. He can go into term insurance, property, burglary and fire insurance to protect his businesses and home.

The best people to sell endowment insurance policy to are civil servants. They can save for their future retirement, insure their lives and as well invest for the education of their children. Life insurance is very versed and they can pick from the many available. So, agents should be careful of the choice of customers they sell policies to at the beginning of their jobs. It determines how much money they are likely to make. Quality customers who are always capable of paying their premiums are the best to target. There is one solid thing agents have to know, "insurance policies are not for the poor".

References

- Ashley, D (2018), How Much Money Does an Independent Insurance Agent Make?, published by Hearst Newspapers LLC, United States

- Rosemary, O (2018), Choosing between Programmed Withdrawal and Annuity, Published by Vanguard Media Limited, Apapa Lagos, Nigeria

Chapter 5

Hard Working and Commitment

There is parallel line between working as an insurance agent and working as a secretary in any office on the planet earth. These are two different kinds of work. When someone works as a secretary, he or she spends most of his or her time in the office taking the necessary record of events through writing. But as an insurance agent, the reverse is the case. An insurance agent also known as insurance salesperson is a field worker.

His own office most of the time is on the street. He is always on the streets except the days he chooses to do some paper work or if the insurance company is attached to any bank. Even those who have attachment to banks sometimes go to the street to meet prospects to sell the services they are instructed to for their financial growth in the company they find themselves.

Choosing and Working as an Insurance Agent

If you are considering finding yourself in any insurance company as a salesperson, just know that you are going there to work. Your own business is to convince prospects who will end up buying insurance products from you. If you are not selling, you are wasting your time in the company. You must put in the needed effort to get the result expected from you by your employers.

An agent eats well because he uses his energy to talk to as many persons as possible. His mouth is his weapon. He convinces people on the services to buy to solve their future needs. In some cases, it may not be what the prospects want but what you want them to buy that will benefit them later in life. For example, many customers may prefer to buy a short term investment products that they will use to save for one year and get their maturity benefit.

But you as an insurance agent having accessed the prospect may find out that what is best for him is a long term investment policy because the person in question is a civil servant. Then you sell the long term policy to him after persuasion and he sees the reason to agree with you. At that point of convincing the prospect to buy the one you feel is fit for his future needs, you advise him on finance management. In that regards, that comes your name as a financial advisor.

5.1 Hard Working as Part of Insurance Salesperson

The term "hard working" is a great deal of effort or endurance. From the definition, it explains that it is not all about putting in efforts in meeting many people on daily basis to buy one or two products. It means that as an agent goes out to meet prospects in the field, he should not conclude so easily when the results are not coming forth immediately. Frankly, a prospect met in the field today by an agent may end up buying after one year of talking to the person. So, hard work and endurance work hand in hand.

According to Cambridge University Press, hard working implies always putting a lot of effort and care into work. The definition from Cambridge university press did not come with the word "effort" but it is matched with care. The product of hard working in insurance sales is results which in other words can be called productions. When an insurance agent work hard on the field and do not apply care, he can lose the business he might have closed to another agent. When an agent meets a prospect in the field, he has to show care to the prospect by always checking on the person. If he does not care, he will lose the business.

There are occasions where agents visited a business shop and on getting to the location found out that their suspect have a baby boy. To show little care, one of the agents carried the baby and played a little with the baby in the shop. The owner who has the baby smiled and felt happy at the attitude displayed by the agent.

Choosing and Working as an Insurance Agent

The agent carried the baby all through their marketing in the business shop. The owner of the shop that the agents came to market their products may not ordinarily buy. But he was moved to buy because of the care shown by one of the agents. The agents ended up marketing burglary and fire insurance services to the shop owner as well as investment for the children's education and he bought. Efforts and care are needed to live a happy life as a salesperson.

Christopher D. Connors of Personal Growth stated, "Well, you'd work hard for something you believe in. You'd work hard for something you've thought and planned for, that will lead you to happiness, success or a well-being (Christopher D. Connors 2017)". From the view of Christopher, hard working gives birth to happiness and success. In the same line, anyone who wants to be a successful insurance salesperson must work hard. When the agent makes it a lifestyle at the job he chooses or about choosing to do, he will definitely be happy when commission is paid to him on the businesses he brought to the insurance company or companies he works for.

Some are not happy when they receive their commission because they did not work hard. Such kinds of agents always apply for other jobs when they are already in an insurance company. They always want to leave because they are not happy with the peanut they receive as commission. It is a problem that many agents are having in insurance companies but someone who is hard working is happy when paid commission of the job he has done.

5.2 Commitment is another Key that keeps Financial Advisors Going

Sometimes financial advisors get tired. They become so weak that they get tired of talking to more people on the streets they find themselves. It appears as if nobody wants to buy insurance services. Imagine talking to about 25 prospects in a week and none of them fills proposal forms and make payments. You begin to ask yourself what you have done wrong. Who did you offend?

Experience of this kind can make a financial advisor feel so cold. It can kill the morale of such agent who finds himself always on the street in search of the right customers that will buy the product the company he works for says he should sell. Only someone who has found his or herself in this kind of state can tell you how frustrating it can be.

But when agents in insurance sales understand this challenge as part of the job, they will not feel weak for a very long time. It is something that does not happen always. It comes and it goes as well. The word "commitment" motivates and keep insurance agents going in the job they signed up to do from their day one.

What is commitment? How has commitment brought about transformation in the lives of many insurance sellers all over the world? Commitment is the state or quality of being dedicated to a cause and activity. It is the state of being faithful to what one believes in or wants. It is the faith that an insurance agent has that he must excel in that his sales because others have been excelling in the same area for years.

Choosing and Working as an Insurance Agent

A successful insurance salesperson is that person who is dedicated in his insurance duties and carried them out diligently. Even when others are talking bad of the company, he sees farer than his current state. He believes that there are better days ahead. Such agent closes his ears to any form of advice that will make him loose focus of his jobs. He loves what he does and believe that even if it does not pay today it will pay tomorrow.

He is like an author who publishes his work independently. He publishes his books through a platform to reach large audience. He writes almost every day of his life to build good book shelves made of many books written by himself. Until he has good audience that reads his books, he never rests.

That is the same thing that makes a good insurance agent. When you are committed, you build yourself in the job. That attitude makes some agents smile in the future. Many agents would have dropped from selling insurance but commitment keeps them going. They believe they will get it right in time to come. They do not quit working.

David Duford speaking on selling final expense insurance stated "Also, one thing one can easily do in this business is, what I call, commitment with full-time effort (David Duford 2015)". When you have your attention given to sales of insurance products, you get the reward of the job. That is not far from the message passed by the owner of an insurance company in United States of America, David Duford.

Choosing and Working as an Insurance Agent

Highly effective insurance agents are committed to achieving their goals, regardless of how many times they fail along the way. If you want to be effective you have to commit and implement. Things may not go as planned, but that doesn't mean your strategy isn't correct. Bold moves can seem like mistakes in the short term, but if you're committed, plow through – dividends don't get paid to the timid (Nathan Bunty 2016).

References

- Cambridge University Press (2018), Hard Working, published by Cambridge University Press, Cambridge, United Kingdom

- Christopher D. Connors (2017), This is What Hard Work is and Why it Matters, published by Medium, United States

- David, D (2015), Selling Final Expense Insurance – The TRUTH, published by David Duford Life Insurance Company, United States

- Nathan, B (2016), 7 Habits of Highly Effective Insurance Agents published by Heritage Insurance Agency, Lancaster, United States

Chapter 6

Disappointment and Negligence by Prospects and People

It is not as if all those that you spoke to will register into your policy. Insurance business does not work like that. So many people will disappoint you as an agent. Many will give you some light excuses even when you have concluded within yourself that you have won the business already.

It is the painful part of the job. So, agents or prospecting agents should take it as part of the job. When disappointed by any prospect that you have built your hope around that he will buy your service no matter what, just move on. Do not stand on that one spot as if he is the only prospect on planet earth.

The funniest part of it is that those prospects that disappointed you at that point you needed them to fill a proposal form and pay their first premium can still come back to you. Many will go and do not return or call you for the sealing of the business. Some are afraid of anything called insurance and because of that need to take their time before they can enter into any contract with any insurance company.

Because some weak insurance companies have disappointed many of their clients when it comes to the time of claiming their money, some prospects disappoint their agents as well. That is a two way thing. But not all will disappoint agents that sweat into the field to work for their daily bread and make ends meet. Disappointment by prospects is one of the challenges we see in the job but that should not make you turn back from being an insurance agent if you have the passion to do the job. You will win because many have been winning.

Nothing good comes easily. So, know that some of the prospects that may disappoint you on the street understand that you are heading into something good. So do not expect to get something good on a platter of gold. There are usually obstacles before you can arrive at the desired destination. That is the nature of the job.

6.1 He gave me Appointment Time but Failed Me

It pains. It weakens agents of insurance companies but that will not make us quit what we do. That job is what puts food on our tables and because of that we cannot say because those prospects disappointed us we quit and resign from the job. That is what makes it an insurance job.

Choosing and Working as an Insurance Agent

The prospect can give you an appointment time to visit his office for the conclusion of the insurance business but end up telling you stories on getting to his office. You think about the money you spent on transport to his office, the time wasted in going to the venue and the rest. You feel like slapping him at that point but you cannot because that is against the work ethics. It is not professional to do such. But no matter what, one quality business you will hit after all the stress will make you smile.

Insurance job is bitter and sweet at the same time. One of the bitter sides is when that young man gives you an appointment to open an insurance policy and on your arrival to his office told you that he used the money he supposed to use in signing into the policy to pay for the child's school fees. You begin to wonder whether the man was normal for telling you that. "He should have told me that the appointment would not hold again", says the agent in his mind. The sweet side of it is when someone you marketed on a service came into your insurance office to enter into insurance contract with the company you work for and pays good premium having you as the financial advisor. You know your commission will really be big and you are happy. That joy makes you do more in the job.

"Am sorry I gave you this appointment time but I changed my mind on that educational policy I wanted to do for my child's future university education". That was the voice of a prospect that ended disappointing a salesperson. "Madam please I still need some time to think about that plan". That was still the voice of the prospect talking to the agent.

After hearing these comments, the agent makes attempt to still convince the prospect but she kept on saying I still need some time. The best thing to do after much effort is to let such person be. It is not all businesses that an agent will close. Some prospects have locked their minds that they would not enter any insurance policies after hearing discouraging stories from people. The "storytellers" will not say where they failed in their own case but continued blaming insurance company. They are painting the image of insurance company in general black.

Even in the midst of all those disappointments, there are better businesses waiting for you outside there. If after disappointment you pressed further and there is no convincing response in return, just move on. There are people outside there that understand insurance that are waiting for you to come and market your products to them.

Life rewards those who take risks and venture forth in hustle mode. Highly effective insurance agents have a sense of urgency about them. They know how to embrace hustle mode when it is necessary (Ryan Hanley 2016). Irrespective of all forms of disappointments insurance agents get from the prospects on the street, those that keep hustling are rewarded.

6.2 Negligence

Some insurance agents are neglected at the beginning of their sales in the market. They look hungry at the beginning but that hunger is the driving force. It is that hunger that keeps a lot of them going even when they have been disappointed by so many people that gave them hope in the past. A successful insurance salesperson said that most successful financial advisors in insurance companies were hungry at the beginning.

If you are a young man selling insurance, in the beginning, people will neglect you. Many ladies will even neglect you when you ask them out. They will say you have no swag and money. That is the fact. But watch what happens after months of working as a salesperson. They will be seeking for your own attention.

What is negligence? It is failure to take proper care over something. Yes, some people may pretend as if you do not exist when you market them on life or non-life businesses. You talk and talk and at the end they will tell you they have heard you.

Some prospects do this to know how you react. Some others do that because that is bad attitude they have. It is their lifestyle. So understand their approach and reactions and create ways to win businesses to yourself irrespective of anything.

Many that neglected can still be interested

As a new sales person in the field, some prospects may think that you are a fake person in the business. They may feel that you are not real and because of that cannot sign any insurance contract with you. Even when you show your identity card to them, they will still not believe. The reason is because there is high rate of fraudulent acts in the society today.

Insurance agents do not find it easy sometimes when they go into the field to do marketing. Many people doubt them especially when they are new faces in the market. This doubt is why some are neglected when they talk to people. Many people being spoken to feel less concerned about the message passed to them by the new salespersons.

But at a point, those persons that neglected you in the beginning can still give you attention. Some can surprisingly visit you in your place of work to know if you are really working as an agent in the company you said you belong. That person who snubbed you when you went into the field to sell your product can engage into a long discussion with you there at the office.

You chat and laugh together and at the end seal the business with good premium. People like that can give the agent many referrals. The person that neglected the agent at the beginning now ends up selling for the agent indirectly.

Choosing and Working as an Insurance Agent

The good thing about getting referrals from people is that the financial advisor (the agent) does not need to talk much. The customer has done the main job in his absence. The work of the agent here is just to go fill proposal form and get the business sealed. Such kind of business is "usually sweet". It does not involve much stress.

When agents visits a particular location for the first time and get neglected, that does not mean no reasonable business can still come out from there. As stated before, those that neglected the agent in their first visit have their reasons. One of the reasons can be because the agents are just dummies. They are new recruits.

As an agent, I have been neglected by staffs in a university library. But after going there for some times, I later got businesses from there. Not just businesses but one was a business with six figure premium. It was a single premium business.

When an agent is neglected in a location and the agent believes that there are people that are capable of buying policies with him in that location, he should not quit. The visit of the agent to that location on many occasions can draw the attention of one or two prospects one day. The visit of the agent is indirect way of telling the people that you are a real agent and not someone that came to steal their money and run away. Once you get one or two customers in that location, many others will follow suit with time. That is the agent that was once neglected by the same people.

Reference

- Ryan Hanley (2016), 7 Habits of Highly Effective Insurance Agents, published by - Agency Nation, Minneapolis, Minnesota, United States

Chapter 7

Customers Relationship Management

Good customers management is an important tool needed in sales for good earnings and happy life as an agent. There are financial advisors that have fewer customers and at the same time make more commissions than those that have more customers. It all centres on good customer management. How do you manage your customers as an agent?

Manage your customers with ease. Grow your business with Salesforce! Close more deals. Make insightful decisions. Accelerate productivity. Get more leads (Sales Force 2019).

Customer relationship management is an approach to manage a company's interaction with current and potential customers. It is specifically focusing on customer retention and ultimately driving sales growth. Every agent that wants to go high in any insurance company must be good at this. It is not as if it is strictly the insurance company that agents work for are the people that pay them but the customers. If you as an agent losses any customer today, know that you have lost some money. So do not play with your customers.

How often do you call them? And how often do you answer their calls when they call you? Do not make the mistake of avoiding the calls placed to you by your customers. They are your strength. They are the reason why you are still paid. The moment your customers stop paying their premiums you stop earning from them.

Call your customers; ask them if there are things they need your attention on. Ask about their children and the well being of the entire family. Tell them that their children are cute and will like to come and visit them anytime you have time. In the course of your care, you are creating more businesses for yourself indirectly. When you make them feel at home with you, they can give you more business contracts. That is the secret.

Your Customers are your Family Members

If you are a good financial advisor, there will be a point it will get to you see some of your good customers as part of your family. They get included in your budget. What they do concerns you. Some of them cannot hold any important occasion without keeping in touch with you.

There will be how you get to some of these customers they begin to like everything about you. What concerns you becomes what concerns them. This is because you people have known each other over the years and they are ready to support you if you are hosting any event.

Some agents in insurance companies have been approached by their customers on personal issues they were facing. These are issues that they could not ordinarily disclose to some other persons but they did that because of the relationship that have existed between them. That is one of the experiences salespersons have when they go out to market their products.

So many agents have built intimacy with their customers over the years. Some have found their life partners in the course of the marketing job. Some got married to the love of their lives through reference by their customers. The job makes you part of the family you were not before. When you are part of the family of your customers, you can sell more products to them at ease.

7.1 Attend occasions of your Customers

Salespersons that want their incomes to keep flowing attend the occasions of their customers. Customers are happy to see their financial advisors present in the events they hold. It gives them the sense that their agents value them.

Agents should not give any form of unnecessary excuses when they are invited by the policyholders they brought into the company. Even if it is an occasion that involves transportation and you know you can afford the transportation money to be there, just try and attend. You can surprise the host who is your customer.

One of the benefits attached to this kind of visit is that the customer may introduce you to the people that matter in the society that are in attendance as well. You can exchange contact with them and brief them later about your job and what you sell. Some of those persons you were introduced to by your customer may buy into your services and pay heavier premium than your customer whom you attended his occasion.

Wisdom is profitable to direct. So, maximize every opportunity you have when you make some visit. It would not be bad if you recover more than the money you spent going to the occasion by getting new prospects that later turn into customers from the occasion. "Activate your brain always". Let it give you avenue to make more money. That is wisdom in action.

If your customers invite you for marriage ceremony, go and celebrate with them. It is a good thing and more doors may be opened for you for better businesses. No one can tell where the breakthrough may come from.

Attend their Baby Dedication

Babies are good gifts from nature. They are good gifts from God. Many have been making efforts to have theirs but have not found. So dedication of a new born baby in church involves sound jubilation.

Choosing and Working as an Insurance Agent

In fact, in this kind of celebration, agents have opportunity to see other parents with their babies. And if the agent specialize in the sales of investment products which involves education insurance products, that can be avenue to establish good contact with parents that attended the dedication. Discussion on where to meet the prospects for the conclusion of the contract continues after the occasion by exchange of contact, and other discussions follow later.

Good insurance agents do not have best time or specific places for marketing of insurance products. They utilize every opportunity they have. They do not wait until it is time for them to go to the field before they can talk to prospects.

Because they know that they make their earnings by opening their mouths to talk to as many customers as possible, they do not close their mouths when there are opportunities to utilize. According to Ekhator Godwin of FBN Insurance, Abraka, Delta state branch, a closed mouth is a closed destiny. Also, an open mouth is an open destiny. In respect to this, insurance agents should speak to people anytime they have the opportunity without any barrier.

There are higher chances of meeting the right customers when agents talk to as many prospects as possible. They should not say that there is no need to talk to people since it is an occasion. Agents should keep advertising what they sell to as many people as possible.

It is not only occasions of joy that agents should attend. When your customers mourn, do that with them. Even during burial ceremony of their loved ones, agents should as well attend. Build that sense of concern towards your customers.

7.2 Proper Policy Monitoring

It is not just about selling some insurance services and then run away. Making money from insurance sales is much bigger than that. Monitoring of customers polices is part of good customer care relationship approach. Good agents in the world of insurance job make sure that the policies they sold to their customers sometime ago are doing well. He makes sure they are active.

How often do your customers pay their premiums? Do you really consider this or you are just good at complaining whenever your commissions are going down. Whenever your commissions are going down, just know that there are some of your customers that are not getting it right again. Some are no longer paying their premiums.

Financial advisors that know what they do check customers' statements of their policies to find out the customers that do not pay their premiums again. After this, they place calls across to such customers. Through the calls, the financial advisors find the reasons behind the lapses and provide solutions and suggestions to the policyholders. Some of them may have forgotten about paying their premiums and such calls placed across to them serve as wake-up calls.

The lasting way to make customers pay premiums effectively is through direct debit. This has been proven over the years of experience in insurance job. Convince your clients to choose this option as their mode of payment. This gives room for automatic payments of customers' premiums. Through this means, the clients get debited from their bank accounts on the debit date they signed up for.

Choosing and Working as an Insurance Agent

The reason for monitoring of the customers polices to make sure that they pay their premiums as of when due is not just because of the commission the agent will get. There are some other reasons behind that. Some policyholders do not really understand insurance in detail.

Among the reason is so that their policies do not lapse. When you remind them that their policies will lapse after none payment for straight three or six months depending on country and the insurance company, it rings bell into their ears. It makes you a good salesperson and also helps the agent wash his hands clean when issue of death benefits come into plan or charges.

In insurance, life insurance looses the death benefits if the policyholder did not pay after some months. In respect to this, the holder when dead will not give the beneficiary the opportunity to claim the death benefit. This has caused many disputes in many insurance offices and the earlier agents bring that to the notice of their customers the better. Agents should manage their clients properly by letting them know of this when they stop paying their premiums as of when due.

On the other hand, insurance companies charge their policyholders when they come for claim after the policy have lapsed due to none payment for months. But it depends on how much the holder has contributed before policy maturity. If the customer contributed good amount of money into any life insurance savings plan, he may not feel the charges because the interest added to the policy at maturity can cover the money charged. Agents of insurance companies should let their clients be aware of these basics when they find out something is likely to go wrong to avoid raising of dust later.

References

- Bain and Company (2015), Management Tools - Customer Relationship Management, published by Bain and Company, 131 Dartmouth Street Boston, Massachusetts 02116, United States

- Ekhator Godwin (2018), Do not take no as an Answer, FBN Insurance, Abraka, Delta State, Nigeria

- Sales Force (2019), Improve sales productivity with the #1 sales app, published by Sales Force Inc, Suite 300, San Francisco, CA 94105, United States

Chapter 8

Marketing, Teamwork, and Evaluation

Marketing is everything you do to place your product or service in the hands of potential customers. It includes diverse disciplines like sales, public relations, pricing, packaging, and distribution (Solomon Kings 2015). Marketing in insurance involves persuading of prospects to go into any insurance contract with the company the agent work with.

Insurance marketing to win customers to the company involves good level of intelligence and understanding. The voices of salespersons are soft and sweet when they are marketing any products to their prospects. From the experience of many customers, some said that good marketers have sugar-coated tongues. In this section, we will discuss marketing of insurance services or products in detail.

There are cases where agents need to apply team work before they can win businesses in a particular area. During presentation to organizations, agents go as a team. Teamwork is the collaborative effort of a team to achieve a common goal or to complete a task in the most effective and efficient way. This concept is seen within the greater framework of a team, which is a group of interdependent individuals who work together towards a common goal (Parker & Glenn 2008).

In working as an insurance agent, there are times when agents need some time to evaluate themselves. This makes them find out whether they are getting it right or wrong in the business of insurance services. Evaluation makes agents to discover and apply new approaches in getting it right in the business.

8.1 The Experience in Marketing Insurance Services

Fake Hope

So many clients will give you hope. Some will make you believe that the deal is already closed. You believe them but all is scam. They are not for real. They just gave you such hope so that you will let them go.

Some are like Trees with Shallow Roots

Agents talk to people on a particular service sold by their companies which are insurance products. At first they have concluded that they will enter into insurance contract. They give the agents just short time to come for the sealing of the business maybe the next day. But it is unfortunate that some of these prospects on getting home changed their minds.

They are like people who received the good news according to the parable of Jesus Christ in the Bible but could not practice them due to obstacles and temptations. Such prospects are happy when they heard about the services marketed to them at first but began to think otherwise when they got home. They have problems with choice of signing into contracts. Agents on meeting the prospects on the appointed date go home angry and disappointed as their hope of closing such deal are thwarted.

There are deals that take much Time

There are customers that take longer time than others before closing of their deals. Some can even take more than one year. They have your contact and one day give you a surprising phone call.

You may not have their contact any longer but they have yours. They call your name and you cannot remember when and where you met them. After discussing with them, they tell you they will visit your office tomorrow. And tomorrow you see them in your office for the closure of the business. These are businesses that you have forgotten long time ago. A customer you marketed a product to today can seal the deal with you in two years.

Choosing and Working as an Insurance Agent

Proposal forms can get Dirty in the Hands of Prospects

There are many prospects that are just good in filling proposal forms handed to insurance salesperson without making payment. Some of these prospects agree at first that they have money to make their first payment before filling forms. But the story changes after they messed up with the form. Some proposal forms are tracked and salespersons account for the forms. No proposal form is acknowledged by any insurer without paying using the policy number written on the proposal form.

The salesperson asks for the money for the first payment. And the prospect be like, oh I don't have money for now. The financial advisor frowns on hearing this. After few push by the agent, he leaves hoping for the prospect to call for payment of their first premium. Some do not call at all. Others keep giving series of excuses until the agent gets tired of calling them.

Some deals are closed at First Meeting

This is the kind of experience every salesperson want to be having always. Nobody likes to be stressed for long. There are prospects that are met in a particular day and the business closed on that same day.

It gives much joy to agents. It makes financial advisors pray to meet such kind of people every day of their lives when they are still insurance agents. Some kinds of people are easy going. They can offer you drinks and even transportation money to go back to your office.

8.2 Strategies to win in Insurance Marketing

Ask Prospects Questions

There are agents that just walk up to prospects and start marketing. It is important to ask prospects few questions when agents meet them to know the products that are likely to suit them at that point in time and from there dig deeper into the products to sell. Asking your prospects questions is good but do not discomfort them with loads of questions.

Some of the questions that agents can ask the prospects are "how is your family sir"? "How is your children sir"? "Please sir where do you work"? These and many other questions can be asked before marketing any product to prospects.

If a prospect says that his children are fine, automatically you know that one of the services to sell to him is educational saving for future higher education. If a prospect gives an answer that he works as a civil servant then the best insurance product to sell to him is retirement insurance products. Questions bring about best products to sell.

People have different plans that fit them at a particular time. So, agents should not be afraid to ask prospects basic questions. It is a helpful approach during marketing. It has helped many agents hit good businesses that changed their lives to better.

Ask for Referrals

After you have sold an insurance product to a client, do not just walk away. Do not feel that you are done with all you need from that customer. There are other things you can gain from him or her. One of those benefits can be referrals from him or her.

Choosing and Working as an Insurance Agent

Referrals can boost your sales and commission in a good way. A client that opened a policy and contributes monthly premium of $18 can give you a client that can be paying monthly premium of $30. There are many already existing customers that have helped agents grow their sales and commissions through referrals. Referrals are good in insurance and salespersons can ask for that from their already existing customers.

Agents can pass the message to their customers like this, "madam since you have started this policy today and you like it, can you help me tell your friends about it for me?" He can make further request by saying, "they do not need to come to our office before they can register. Once you tell anyone and he or she agrees, just call me or alert me, I can go meet the person in any place he or she is for proper signing into the contract". The customer agrees but you have to keep checking on him or her often.

There are some customers that are business minded. Some would not like to refer someone without being motivated. They sometimes ask the agents, "how much will you give to me if I give you customers". Smart agents enter into business deals with such clients. They may say, I will give you $3 for any customer that can enter into long term life insurance plan and pay a minimum of $100 as the monthly premium. Some customers sometimes agree and then give salespersons customers and get their pay for each person they refer.

Persistent and Follow-up

Some customers sometimes behave as if they are careless with the plan you introduced them into. Many just want to know how serious you are with the service you sell. After many times of persistency, many end up doing what you tell them to go into some time ago.

Do not get tired immediately a prospect tells you that he does not like the plans that the insurance company you work with sells. You need to convince such prospect. Give him reasons why he needs to sign into that contract. Enlighten him the more on that plan as far as he gives you listening ear.

Do not take no as an answer from prospects (Ekhator Godwin 2018). According to Ekhator Godwin of FBN Insurance, you do not just leave a prospect to go once he said that he cannot pick any insurance policy. He made it clear that a smart agent do not just stop convincing the prospect even when the prospect said no.

Agents that want to succeed in marketing always follow up with their prospects until they get the fruit of the marketing. The fruit of the marketing is closing of businesses. She calls often to know when and where the prospect prefers for the sealing of businesses. Some prospects get tired at answering agents calls. They end up registering into the policies.

8.3 Teamwork of agents

New agents in insurance companies need to work with others that have been in insurance for some time. The most successful businesses strive for a teamwork culture where everyone has an important role to play and everyone fits into the overall whole. That is how it is when agents work today in some occasions. This results to combination of ideas that will give good result.

Knowledgeable accumulation and sharing is important. When different salespersons visit some locations for presentation and selling of insurance services, they pass knowledge into the prospects they talk to. It makes their presentation to have weight and well honoured. It is not every locations that one single agent goes to and make some sales.

There are places that they need to go as a team. When speaking to large number of persons, it is good to go in group. Doing so will make them cover and talk to as many people as possible.

Sometimes, they share the topics they are to educate the people on individually for in-depth study. Each agent goes and study the particular area assigned to him or her. So on the day of the presentation to larger number of people, each of the agents becomes a professional in their own field of expertise. Team is needed in some cases in marketing of insurance products.

As human body is, different parts perform specific functions. That is what it entails when agents go out in group to storm a particular location or locations. They divide the functions.

8.4 Evaluation

The word evaluation means "the making of a judgement about the amount, number, or value of something; assessment". It is a good thing for salespersons to evaluate themselves in the course of doing their insurance jobs. This assessment will help agents determine what work best for them and what do not work at all. The location they make sales the more, the people that buy most from them, the product that give them more return and the rest.

Every successful insurance agent sits down once in a while for proper evaluation. How many productions do I have this week and how heavy is the premium? If after the analysis you discovered that you do not have much, you can think of the next step to take.

The choice may be on how to approach newer prospects and how to talk to them to pay higher premiums. Maybe it happens that when the customers ask you how much is the minimum premium, you easily tell them $14. The new evaluation can make you have another approach of asking the prospects how much they want to be paying monthly as premiums for those that opted in for payment of their premiums monthly. Some will choose to be paying more than the least premium provided by the company if you ask them such question. And the higher the premium they pay, the higher your commission.

Choosing and Working as an Insurance Agent

Again, after evaluation on your previous performance, you can detect the people that likely buy into the insurance services you sell the more. This will make you have maximum utility of your time. You concentrate more on such people and save yourself the stress of wasting your energy on some kind of people. If civil servants are the people that buy most insurance services than businessmen and women after your analysis, you go for them.

References

- Montebello, Anthony; Buzzotta and Victor (1993), Work Teams That Work, published by Questia, Chicago, United States

- Parker, Glenn (2008), Team Players and Teamwork: New Strategies for Developing Successful Collaboration, San Francisco: Jossey-Bass. pp. 1–68. ISBN 978-0-787-99811-0.

- Salas, Eduardo, Nancy J. Cooke, and Michael A. Rosen (2008), On Teams, Teamwork, as well as Team Performance: Discoveries and Developments, published by The Journal of the Human Factors and Ergonomics Society, Washington, DC, United States

- Solomon Kings (2015), Marketing of Insurance Services (problems and Prospect), published by Afribary, Enugu, Nigeria

Chapter 9

Selling rightly, Benefits, and Comparison with Bank Job

There are many insurance agents that have painted the image of the company they work with black due to miss selling. Because many are anxious to make sales, they sell wrongly. Some before maturity of their clients policies are afraid as they do not know how to go back to the customers they miss sold to make peace. Agents are good at miss selling because they want to have huge commissions.

There are benefits attached when a financial advisor sells the services he is instructed to sell rightly. One of those benefits is that the agent will have peace of mind. Another is that it saves the agent from the shame of being embarrassed due to miss selling. New agents in insurance job should endeavour to sell their products rightly. Do not lie to any customer because it may be disastrous when the customer finds out the truth about the policy.

In working as insurance agent, there are benefit one stands to get. These benefits you may not get from any other salary paying jobs. We will discuss these benefits in detail under a separate subheading.

Insurance and banking are included under the same genre in some areas. They are all under finance. Because of being in the same category, there are banks that also have and manage insurance companies. In this chapter, what to be covered as well is the comparison between insurance and banking. These are two different jobs with different approach for survival in them. The comparison will help you understand more or better.

9.1 Selling Rightly as an Insurance Agent

Everyone wants to make money. People want to live a more comfortable life. They want to smile always and be praised by people around them. Because of this, they do many dirty things which ordinarily they would not like to do. The same applies to insurance agents all over the world.

Because they do not want to receive few dollars as their commission every month, they devise ways for their survival. They do not want to gradually grow. All they want is to build their commissions overnight. Agents think that it is sharpness but little do they know they are putting themselves into trouble. Until they miss sell to a no nonsense person, their legs are brought out to the public.

Why increasing the duration given to you by your customer at the initiation of the contract? Your customer told you that he is entering the contract for five years and you write ten years in the proposal form because you want your commission to be high when paid. That is insincerity and deception.

Choosing and Working as an Insurance Agent

What happens to the customer when he comes for maturity at the end of the five years? The technical administrator tells him that his policy will mature in 10 years and not 5 years again. What it implies is that he cannot claim all his maturity benefit at that point in time. The customer narrates that he opted in to the contract for 5 years and not 10 as stated in the system and the technical administrator states that he sees 10 years and not 5 years.

The customer says he needs the money and that results to strong argument in the insurance office. It is very disappointing when one hopes to do something with his money and he is told another story at the end. That is usually very painful. You will understand better if you have found yourself in that condition. Maybe the customer has already plan to buy a land with the money to be claimed at exactly 5 years at the supposed maturity and now he is hearing 10 years.

What a life? What a disaster that can "light fire" in the insurance office. So he has to wait for extra five years before he can claim the money for the land he wants to buy at exactly five years? If the customer chooses to take what he has saved under the investment policy at that point in time, it becomes termination. It is termination because the system states that the plan was queued in to run for 10 years and not five years.

And if the customer goes ahead and terminates, he will lose some of the benefits in the plan. Also, he may lose some part of his invested money but all depends on how the plan is designed by the company. This is how many agents have made insurance companies loose integrity in the eyes of people.

Choosing and Working as an Insurance Agent

How will the customer see the same agent that sold the insurance service to him? Do you think the same agent can freely market to other people in the place where or office where the person he miss sold to is? Big time disappointment!

In fact, the deceived customer would have already told the people around him not to buy anything insurance services from your company before your arrival. Also, you as an agent will not even feel free to say anything about what you sell the moment you see the customer you hurt before due to miss selling.

Not selling rightly has made many agents find themselves in police custody cells. Some stay in the custody until they reach an agreement with the customer they miss sold to. Some agree to balance the customer the short paid claim after termination which supposed to be maturity.

Agents have to be wise when they sell to the people outside there. For dummies (beginners) that are into insurance sales, some unit managers are not straight forward. Some of them push the agents to increase the duration for policies maturity which is against the wish of the customer. The reason they do this is because they also want to receive high commissions. If your commission is high, that of your unit manager becomes high as well. That is how insurance works.

Choosing and Working as an Insurance Agent

Sell rightly to maintain steady Growth

When an agent sells rightly, he or she maintains steady growth in his or her job with peace of mind. The growth comes because when you sell right to someone and the person claims the maturity benefit at the end of maturity happily, the customer can refer you to someone else. But when it is the other way round, the financial advisor paints the image black and looses customer.

Agents that sell right may not have fast growth at the beginning of their career as insurance salespersons. But when people that have sold today get their maturity benefits at the due time, they become happy and spread the good news to the others. Selling right as insurance agent helps you maintain clean sheet and you feel happy as you ascend in your commission because you always stay clean and nobody disturbs you due to miss selling.

Effects of not selling rightly as an Insurance Agent

Fear of termination

When you as an agent do not sell rightly to any customer of yours, you are always afraid of the customer coming to terminate the policy. Because the policy states that the minimum duration for maturity is five years and you told the customer he can claim his money at the second year because you want to make sales, your mind flies whenever the customer tells you that two years will soon complete and he will like to have his claim at that time. The agent has sleepless nights because he knows he may be in trouble if the customer is a no nonsense person.

Fear of Query

There are lies or miss selling that when it gets to the ears of the head office of the insurance company can result to issuing of query to the agent. Query is a question about something, especially in order to express one's doubts about it or to check its validity or accuracy. When query is issued from head office to an agent to ask of the report against him, the head office takes note of the query.

If not answered convincingly by the receiver, he may get himself into trouble. When query on similar issue is issued again to the same agent for many times, it becomes clear that elements of truth exist on the accusations against the agent. Queries can prevent an agent from being promoted to higher positions in insurance companies.

Sacking of Agents

Agents that miss sell to customers are likely to be sacked depending on the magnitude of their offense. Some after receiving series of queries on one particular issue are sacked after invitation and interrogation by the head office. It is disgraceful but insurers take such action.

Some promise customers interest of 50% after investing in their endowment plans. The interest given by agents is usually far higher than the one approved by the insurance company. Some agents have been sacked due to such offense. Many agents that have been sacked by the company they worked with as a result of miss selling are floating today. Many are struggling to find good jobs to continue living as humans.

Embarrassment

If an agent does not sale rightly to customers, he can get embarrassed. This embarrassment can take place in the agent's office or even along roads. There have been cases where insurance salespersons were fought on the road by customers that terminated their policies due to miss selling. The customer met the agent in supermarket and began to quarrel with him which resulted to fight.

What kind of embarrassment is bigger than when your own customers you are to give financial advises hand you over to the police? Not only that but also have you put in police custody cell. That is shameful. It is a negative effect of miss selling to customers. Agents should sell rightly to avoid problems.

9.2 Benefits of working as Insurance Agent

As an insurance salesperson, there are benefits that you will enjoy that other fixed salary workers do not enjoy. The job has some unique outstanding features. There are things that a financial advisor can do on his own that a worker in bank and other offices cannot do. In this sentence, we will be discussing in detail the benefits of working as an insurance agent.

Freedom

There is freedom of movement and decisions when one works as insurance salesperson. Agents sometimes are not held by the rule that they must be in the office at a particular time to attend to customers unlike cashiers in banks that are mandate to be at work at a particular time. Agents are free and are not under pressure when it comes to time for them to resume work.

They work with appointment time given to them by their prospects and clients. These clients can tell the agents to meet them at the office by 12pm and they make sure that they are there at that point in time. Also, the prospect can invite the financial advisor to a hotel. He goes there and the man order foods and drinks and they enjoy together as they seal insurance contract.

Opportunity to meet Dignitaries

Dignitaries are persons considered to be important because of high rank or office. They are respected men in the society. They are the people whose words are heavy and heard by the society. Dignitaries through their positions make things happen.

Working as salesperson gives you the ability to meet these people in one way or the other. Bold financial advisors enter offices of people that hold top positions to make sales. These are the people with the money and they can pay heavy premiums. Some of the premiums can change the lives of advisors when commissions are paid on such businesses.

Sometimes, agents are prevented from seeing these people but the smart ones still find their ways into the offices. They sometimes strike deals with the receptionists just for them to let them see the dignitaries. Some agents claim to have important appointment with the dignitaries which cannot be disclosed just because they want to meet the people that matter. But there is no appointment. They make such claim just for them to be able to see the men or women of high class.

Choosing and Working as an Insurance Agent

Some of these dignitaries have given many salespersons lift in their jobs. Some with their powers and positions have instructed and advised other staff to register into the insurance plans sold by the agents. A situation whereby a dignitary gives an agent about 60 new capable customers, they agent becomes happy because he has already seen his growth. Some dignitaries have become friends with financial advisors because of the kind of jobs the advisors do.

Ability to do other businesses

Insurance job is not like other jobs that tie people down in one particular place. Here, you can be a salesperson and still do other things. You can work as salesperson and also have other businesses running outside there. These businesses outside there give you opportunities to earn more money.

You have the opportunity to supervise these businesses at your own time. You can go out for marketing and on your way back stop by to check on how your boys or girls are selling. You continue with your job after staying in your shop for some time.

Limitless Earnings

You do not have limit on how much you earn when you work as an insurance salesperson. Blank check is given to people that work in this area of specialization. They determine how much they want to take home towards the end of every month. People sit down and work for 8 hours, and at the end of the month have fixed payment which is much lower than what insurance salespersons take home.

Choosing and Working as an Insurance Agent

An insurance financial advisor can go home with strong six digits earning every month while someone that works for salary manages five digits earning. There are outstanding agents in risk management profession that steadily earn seven digits. The job pays high for those that are dedicated, focused and productive. The money made by an agent in a month can cover six months salaries of a worker that is on fixed salary.

Payments within short times

There are many workers whose pay come at the last day of the month when the employees have waited for a long time. This is quite different from the way workers are paid in insurance companies. Payment to agents in insurance industry comes quick. Salespersons receive their pays on time and use their pay to plan their lives on time.

Also, some insurance companies pay two times in a month. Some pay their agents allowances first before commission. The allowances cover the transportation and other fees that the agents need while in the field marketing. Sometimes, agents do not use all the money for that which they are made for but it depends on how the insurance company operate. For example, in insurance company that is a subsidiary of a bank, the agents do not go out most times for marketing. They stay inside the banking halls and market to customers that enter the halls on insurance products.

A typical example is that of First Bank of Nigeria Insurance (FBN Insurance). Here, most agents do not go out for marketing. In respect to this, they do not spend most of the allowance paid to them on transportation. They spend the money on their basic needs like what commission is paid to them cover.

Sometimes, insurance companies pay three times in a month. These payments are allowance, commission, and supplementary. Supplementary are paid to agents as commissions that have not been paid to them before on premiums paid by policyholders sometime ago. Supplementary can come due to late payment of premiums by customers and sometimes as a result of late capturing and conversation by technical administrators.

9.3 Bank Staff Salaries versus Insurance Agents

As stated before, there are some banks that have insurance companies as well. Though they are different subsidiaries but they work under one holding. The bankers sometimes feel they earn more money than the agents while some agents feel otherwise. Here, we are going to compare the earnings of these two groups of people.

1. Bankers are on fixed salary while the agents earn by commission.

2. Bank officials money does not grow gradually but insurance agents who know what they are doing in the business have growth in their commission gradually.

3. Bank officials mostly earn more than financial advisors when the advisors just started the job newly.

4. Overtime, insurance agents earn more than bank officials. This is because as they have more customers the more they grow their earnings.

4. Sometimes, the earning of agents can be discouragingly low when there is error in the device used for the calculation of the commission while bankers maintain their constant fixed salaries.

5. Sometimes, insurance agents hardly lack money because they are paid two and at times three times in a month while bank officials are paid once in a month, and can spend such money fast which may make them to borrow.

6. A good single premium business of an insurance agent can give the agent sound commission that can be enough to pay five bank officials in a month.

Contact the Author

The author needs your feedback. If you want to contact him on some other topics not discussed in the book, you can reach him through any of these channels:

- ➤ Email: pmicheal2013@gmail.com
- ➤ Phone number: +2347037278694

Other Books written by the Author

- ➤ Basic Information in Youth and Youth Empowerment
- ➤ Powder Metallurgy: Its Engineering Consideration and Applications on Copper
- ➤ Metallurgical and Materials Engineering: Introduction and Applications
- ➤ Premarital Sex: Causes, Effects and Remedies
- ➤ Guide to Youth Challenges
- ➤ Nigerian Youth Challenges
- ➤ Understanding the usefulness of Computer in the Twenty-first Century

All the above books are available in online book stores. Search for them through Google or other search engines.

www.ingramcontent.com/pod-product-compliance
Lightning Source LLC
Chambersburg PA
CBHW072200170526
45158CB00004BB/1711

Links to the Author's online Pages

- ➤ https://amazon.com/author/uzochukwup
- ➤ http://www.lulu.com/spotlight/uzochukwumikep